THE STORY OF NAPOLEON

NAPOLEON AS A BOY

THE CHILDREN'S HEROES SERIES

THE STORY OF
NAPOLEON

BY

H. E. MARSHALL

*WITH PICTURES
BY ALLAN STEWART*

YESTERDAY'S CLASSICS

CHAPEL HILL, NORTH CAROLINA

This edition, first published in 2007 by Yesterday's Classics, an imprint of Yesterday's Classics, LLC, is an unabridged republication of the work originally published by T. C. & E. C. Jack Ltd. in 1908. For a listing of the books that are published by Yesterday's Classics, please visit www.yesterdaysclassics.com. Yesterday's Classics is the publishing arm of the Baldwin Online Children's Literature Project which presents the complete text of hundreds of classic books for children at www.mainlesson.com.

ISBN-10: 1-59915-214-2
ISBN-13: 978-1-59915-214-1

Yesterday's Classics, LLC
PO Box 3418
Chapel Hill, NC 27515

To

MALCOLM

PREFACE

EACH of us bears about within him a dark, strange room, through the closed doors of which none but himself and God may pass to see and know what lies therein. With some the room is small, and much is left without for all the world to see and know. With some the room is very large, shutting in perchance the whole true man. And when we meet with such an one, and ask ourselves if he be great or little, good or bad, we must, if we be honest, say "I know not, for I cannot understand."

Such was the great Napoleon. The strange dark room he bore within was very large. And though there be many who hold aloft a flaming torch, and cry, "Come, follow me, and I will show to you what lay in that dark place," in smoke and flare the light dies out, the darkness seems yet darker, and we know as little.

So, if you ask me is this Napoleon a true hero, I say, God—who alone has seen and knows what lay in that dark room—God knows.

H.E. MARSHALL.

OXFORD.

CONTENTS

CHAPTER I

NAPOLEON AT SCHOOL

TO the south of Europe there is a sunny blue sea called the Mediterranean.

In this sunny, blue sea about fifty miles from the coast of Italy lies the island of Corsica, a rugged and beautiful little island, full of mountains. Its people are hardy and brave, and, like all mountain peoples, they love liberty. But for hundreds of years the island belonged to the Republic of Genoa. The people hated to be ruled by Genoa, and at last, under a leader called Paoli, they rebelled and fought for freedom—fought indeed so well that they nearly drove the Genoese out. Then the Genoese asked the French to help them, and at last, tired of the struggle, they sold the island to France.

At that the Corsicans were very angry. What right had the Genoese to sell them like cattle to a new master? they asked. So they went on fighting the French, as they had fought the Genoese.

Among those who fought were Charles-Marie Bonaparte and his brave wife, Letizia. Bonaparte was an Italian, but for many years his family had lived in

Corsica. He was a noble; but in Corsica there was little difference between nobles and shepherds—they were all poor and proud alike. Letizia was young and beautiful, yet she bore all the hardships of war bravely. She followed her husband even to the battle-field. She was often in danger from flying bullets, yet she feared nothing, and thought only of the safety of her husband and the freedom of her country. By mountain paths, steep and narrow; through trackless forests, called in Corsica, "maquis"; over streams where there were no bridges, Letizia followed her husband. She was only a girl, but she had the heart of a hero, and not until the struggle proved hopeless did she give in.

For France was great and Corsica little, and brave though the people were, they were at last forced to yield; their island became part of the French dominion, and their leader Paoli fled over the seas.

And here, in this little isle, almost before the roar of battle had ceased, among a people full of sullen anger and bitterness against their conquerors, one blazing August day in 1769 a little son was born to Charles and Letizia Bonaparte. They gave him the name of Napoleon, a name which he was to make famous all the world over, and for all time to come.

Napoleon had several brothers and sisters, and their mother, having only one servant, had little time to look after the children. So she gave them a big, empty room in which to play. The walls and floor of this room were bare, and there was nothing in it except the children's toys. Here they were allowed to do as they liked. They scribbled and drew pictures on the walls, and played at all sorts of games. Napoleon always drew soldiers marching to battle, and he played with nothing but a drum and a wooden sword. He used to get up battles, too, amongst the boys of the neighbourhood. The wars would last for months at a time, during which there would be many fierce fights, surprises, and assaults. Napoleon was always leader, and made the others obey him. He was afraid of no one, and he bit, scratched, and slapped any one, big or little, as he chose. He was often noisy and quarrelsome, and bullied his brothers and sisters, especially Joseph, who was older than he.

But at times, even when he was a very small boy, he would be moody and thoughtful, and would walk about by himself, refusing to speak or play with the others. He was an untidy little boy, not caring in the least how he was dressed. Straight dark hair straggled over his brown face, his stockings hung down over his shoe-tops, and altogether he must have looked a wild little harum-scarum.

When Napoleon was about five years old he was sent to a school for little girls kept by nuns. But he did not stay long there and was soon sent to a boys' school, with his brother Joseph. Here the boys in class were set opposite each other in two rows, each under a large flag. One was the flag of Carthage, the other the flag of Rome, with S.P.Q.R. upon it, which means "Senatus Populusque Romanus." That is Latin for "The Senate and People of Rome."

The boys were arranged like this so that each side might try to learn better than the other, and fight

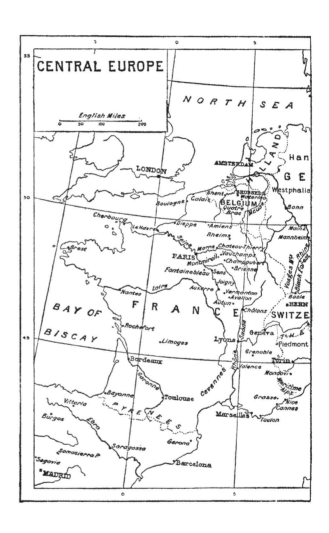

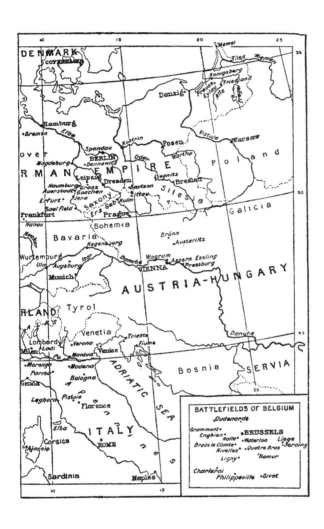

and conquer in lessons, as the Romans and Carthaginians fought in war.

As Napoleon was the younger of the two brothers, he was put on the side of Carthage. But he did not like that at all, for in history he knew the Romans had always been the conquerors, and he liked to be on the winning side. So Joseph, who did not mind so much, changed with Napoleon, and allowed him to be a Roman.

Napoleon loved soldiers better than anything else and he longed to be one. Every morning, before he went to school, he was given a piece of white bread. This he used to give to a soldier in exchange for a piece of coarse brown bread. His mother was not very pleased at this. "Why do you give away your good white bread for a piece of brown?" she asked him one day.

"Because," replied Napoleon, "if I am going to be a soldier I must get used to eating soldiers' bread. Besides, I like it."

As he loved soldiers so much, his father and mother decided that he should be one. And one December day a little ship sailed away from Corsica, carrying Charles Bonaparte and his two sons, Joseph and Napoleon, over the sea to France. Napoleon was not yet ten, and Joseph scarcely a year older. He was going to learn to be a priest, and Napoleon to be a soldier.

The boys were sent to school at a town called Autun. With his fellows Joseph soon became a favourite. He was a little shy at first, but he was lively and gay, and joined in games with the other boys.

Napoleon, on the other hand, was silent and sad. His dark face looked sulky, and instead of joining in the games, he liked best to go about by himself. So the boys teased him. They called him "cowardly Corsican," and reminded him that his island had been conquered by the French. At first Napoleon paid no attention. Then suddenly, one day, flashing round on his tormentors, he cried, "If the French had been four against one only, they would never have had Corsica: but they were ten to one."

But if Joseph was the greater favourite, Napoleon was far the more clever. He soon learned to read and speak in French. For to the boys French was a foreign language; at home, in Corsica, they spoke Italian. But although Napoleon learned to speak French very well, all his life long he made mistakes in it, especially in writing. He wrote very badly too—to hide his bad spelling, some people say.

The little, sulky, lonely boy did not stay long at Autun. In about three months his father came to take him away to the military school at Brienne. But Joseph was to be left at Autun. The two brothers had never before been parted, and although Napoleon bullied Joseph they were very fond of each other. Now that they were in a strange land, far from their home, among people speaking a strange language, they seemed to love each other more. When they knew that they must part, Joseph burst into tears. But Napoleon tried hard to pretend that he did not care. His dark

NAPOLEON AS A BOY

face only looked more sulky than before. But although he tried hard, he could not quite keep back the tears, and one slowly trickled down his cheek.

At first Napoleon was not happy at his new school, even though he was dressed in a uniform and was going to be a soldier. He was dreadfully home-sick. He was told that he would have to stay at school for six years, and to a little boy of nine it seemed as if six years would never end.

As Napoleon was shy, moody, and silent, his schoolfellows teased him here too. They nicknamed him "Straw on Nose," because they thought that he held his nose in the air, and that Napoleon sounded like the French words for straw on nose—"la paille au nez." They teased him, also, about his country. "You are a conquered nation, a people of slaves," they said.

But one winter, when Napoleon had been about four years at school, the boys had lessons about the building of ramparts and fortifications. They were taught the names of the different kinds of forts, their uses, and how best to attack and defend them. While these lessons were going on, there came a heavy fall of snow. This gave Napoleon a grand idea. He proposed that they should build a fortress of snow, and attack and defend it like soldiers.

All the boys were delighted with the idea. Napoleon drew out the lines of the fort, and soon every one was hard at work with spade and wheel-barrow, eagerly building under Napoleon's directions.

When the fort was finished, the boys took sides, and fought with snowballs. Napoleon was general, and he commanded both sides, giving orders sometimes to the besiegers, sometimes to the defenders. The masters were quite pleased, and looked on, cheering those boys who showed most courage and cleverness.

Soon the fame of the fort spread far, and people came from all round about to see it and watch the fights. These went on as long as the snow lay upon the ground. But at last March came, the sun began to grow warm, the snow melted, and the storming and snow-balling came to an end. The masters were not sorry when this happened, as many of the boys had caught bad colds from playing so much in the snow. As for Napoleon, he was more sure than ever that the life of a soldier was the grandest possible, and he felt that he was born to make others obey him.

As to his lessons, Napoleon learned no Greek, and never did his Latin well. He loved the tales of the Greek and Roman heroes, but he read them in translations. It seemed to him waste of time to try to read them in a dead or foreign language. At arithmetic and geometry he was good. He liked his geography lessons too, but above all he loved history. Whenever he had a spare moment he might be found reading, and it was history and the lives of great men that he read. Indeed he often read when he ought to have been playing games. So he never grew tall; and although his shoulders were broad, he was thin and delicate-looking.

CHAPTER II

NAPOLEON AN OFFICER

There was still another year to pass in Brienne, Napoleon thought. But one day he was told that he had been admitted to the military school at Paris. And on the 30th of October 1784 he set out for the capital with four other boys.

At Paris Napoleon was in his element. It seemed to him that he was no longer at school, but in a city under arms and in a state of war. All around him he saw men in uniforms. He was no longer awakened from sleep or called to class by the sound of a bell, but by the rat-tat of a drum. Sentinels marched to and fro. Every hour, by night or day, he heard the sharp word of command, the ring and thud of grounding muskets. All the talk was of war, and the boys discussed together the regiments to which they would belong, their uniforms, and arms.

When Napoleon had been a year in Paris he passed his examinations, and received his commission as second lieutenant in the artillery regiment of La Fère, one of the finest in the army, and on the 30th of October 1785 he and another boy set out to join their regiment at Valence. They were only boys of sixteen and seventeen, but they felt very grand, for now they were real officers. They wore swords and belts and silver collar-clasps. But to their great grief they were not yet allowed to wear the uniform of their regiment, but had to travel in their school uniforms. Still, it was a fine thing to wear a sword. So they climbed joyfully into the Lyons coach, and were soon whirling away southwards behind spanking horses.

The La Fère regiment, being one of the best, was one of the most hard-working of the French artillery. The men got up early, and worked hard at marching, drilling, and shooting. Napoleon was in a way still a pupil. He had to begin at the bottom, to serve first as a gunner, then as corporal and sergeant, so that he might know his work in every detail. Then only was he considered fit to be an officer.

Besides drilling and studying gunnery, he read everything he could about soldiers and about war. He learned, too, to draw maps and plans, and as he was one of the keenest, soon became one of the best, of the officers of the regiment.

But he did not spend all his time in work; he often went home on leave. He had his share too in all the fun and jokes of which his companions were fond. He took part in dinners, balls, and parties. Indeed since he had become an officer, Napoleon was no longer the moody boy he had been, although at times he might have fits of passion.

But meanwhile, as the days and months went on, great changes were taking place in France.

At this time the position of King and people in France was very different from what it was in Britain. The people, of Britain, through long years of struggle, had gained freedom. There they lived under what is called a limited monarchy; that is, the power of the King was held in check by Lords and Commons. But in France there was no check upon the King. He could do as he liked. Under him, there were the "three estates"—that is, the nobles, the clergy, and the people. The nobles and the clergy paid no taxes. They were called the privileged classes. They and the King spent a great deal of money. So the third estate—that is, the people—had to pay. Every year the King and nobles spent more and more. Every year the people had to pay more and more.

As the years went on the people grew more and more miserable, and more and more weary of their rulers. Many of them were very ignorant. They hardly knew what was wrong, or how it might be put right. They only knew that they were poor, miserable, and hungry. Riots grew frequent; all the summer of 1789 was stormy with them. At last the people broke out fiercely in Paris. They seized and pulled down the state prison. The King was powerless. "It is revolt," said he, when he heard of it.

"Nay, sire," replied his minister, "it is revolution."

Soon all over France revolution was blazing. The King was driven from the throne. Everything was turned topsy-turvy, and men knew not whom to follow.

But Napoleon was no Frenchman. He was a Corsican. The troubles of France did not touch him, except that he thought perhaps out of them good might come to his dear island. And so in this time of wild unrest he asked for leave and went home.

For the next four years Napoleon divided his time between France and Corsica.

Corsica, like France, was in a state of turmoil and anarchy. Paoli, the great Corsican hero, had returned from exile, and was everywhere greeted with cheers.

When a boy Napoleon had loved and honoured Paoli. But soon these two, the grey old hero whose work was done, and the brown-faced lad whose work was only beginning, quarrelled. The story of these quarrels is hard to follow, but at last Napoleon, who had been a great patriot, took the side of France. Then he and all his family were forced to flee from Corsica in secret, and after many adventures they arrived safely in Marseilles. There Napoleon left his mother and sisters in great poverty, and went to join his regiment, which was now at Nice. From henceforth he was a Frenchman.

When the French rebelled against their King, many of the princes and rulers of the other countries of Europe joined together and threatened to make war against France, unless the French people placed Louis upon the throne again.

At first Britain did not openly join with the others. But in January 1793 the French put their King to death, and a few weeks after Britain joined the allies.

Even some of the French themselves joined them, so that France had to fight a civil war as well as one against foreign enemies.

Among the French who helped the allies, and who were helped by them, were the people of Toulon. An army of the allies took possession of the fortress, and a squadron of British ships lay in the harbour, while the French Revolutionary army besieged the town.

Napoleon now joined this army as commander of artillery, and it is from the siege of Toulon that his fame as a soldier dates. It is said by some, indeed, that the taking of the town was almost entirely due to him, but others think that his part in it was really very small.

However that may be, when Napoleon arrived at Toulon the army was badly officered, and there was hardly any artillery at all. He at once set eagerly to work, and in a few days he had forty cannon and everything needed for the building of new forts. He gathered shot and shell, too, and built forts and batteries. He wrote, ordered, and fought unceasingly.

For weeks, the siege went on. There were attacks and counter-attacks, assaults, and sallies, and at last a fort called L'Eguillette was taken. "To-morrow, or the day after, we shall sup in Toulon," said Napoleon.

And he was right. The British ships made ready to sail away. The people of Toulon were seized with panic. The British ships were their last and only hope. Nothing else could save them from falling into the hands of the terrible revolutionists, so they made ready to go with them. Soon the sea was crowded with boats carrying terror-stricken men, women, and children to the fleet. In their haste many were drowned, sometimes whole boat-loads being overturned by the too eager crowds.

All day the flight lasted. Then about nine o'clock in the evening a terrible explosion shook the earth. The sea seemed to belch forth fire, the dark night was suddenly bright as day, and horrible with noise and smoke. Fierce red flames licked the sky, and black against the lurid light, showed the shattered hulks of ships. It was the British commander who, before leaving, had set fire to a great part of the arsenal and blown up about a dozen French ships of war.

The siege was over, and next day the victorious troops marched into the now almost silent and deserted town.

Napoleon by this time had many good friends among the men who were ruling France, and it seemed as if his fortune was made. But these were very wild and uncertain times. His friends fell into disgrace, Napoleon himself was put into prison for a short time, and at last we find him once more, poor and lonely, wandering the streets of Paris, with nothing to do.

But it was now, when he, seemed forgotten and cast aside, that his great chance came to him.

France, besides having to fight outside enemies, was full of unrest and discontent within its borders. The people were tired of the Convention, as the Government was now called, and wished to overthrow

THE LITTLE CORSICAN OFFICER

its power. At last the citizens of Paris took up arms, and resolved to attack the palace of the Tuileries.

The members of the Convention then gathered to consult. They knew that their danger was great. They must do something quickly, if they were not to be overthrown. But who was to lead their soldiers.

Suddenly one of their number called Barras rose. "I know the man whom you want," he said. "He is a little Corsican officer who will not stand on ceremony."

So Napoleon was sent for.

It was by this time late at night. But Napoleon began to work at once, and by six o'clock next morning every street leading to the Tuileries was guarded with cannon.

The rioters had no cannon, but they were well armed with muskets, and thirty thousand of them came crowding along the narrow streets to besiege the palace.

For many hours the two forces stood facing each other, neither exchanging a shot; but at last, about half-past four, some one fired. It was a signal for all to begin. Napoleon's cannon swept the streets. The rioters fled before the hail of grape-shot, leaving their dead upon the ground. By six in the evening all was quiet again. Thanks to "the little Corsican," the Convention had won. And Napoleon had gained for himself the post of commander-in-chief of the army of the Interior.

One day very soon after this a boy of about twelve asked to see Napoleon. The boy's name was Eugène Beauharnais, and with tears in his eyes he told Napoleon that his father had been a soldier. He had fought for the Republic, but had been killed. Now Eugène came to beg for his father's sword.

Napoleon was sorry for the boy, and ordered at once that the sword should be given to him. As soon as Eugène saw it he seized it, kissed it, and carried it away happy.

The next day, Eugène's mother, who was a very beautiful lady, came to thank Napoleon for having been so kind to her boy. Soon Napoleon began to love this beautiful lady, although she was many years older than he. She loved him too, and in a short time they were married.

So in a few months, from being almost penniless and unknown, Napoleon had become famous and well off, and had married a fine lady, who was able to make friends for him among the rulers of the land.

But Josephine de Beauharnais had married a great man, or rather, a man who was going to be great, and a few days after the wedding they had to say good-bye to each other. For among the Alps there was still fighting, and Napoleon was ordered off to take command of the army of Italy.

It will not be possible to follow Napoleon through all his battles. He had to fight two armies—one Austrian and one Sardinian. Against so strong an enemy he knew that his only hope was in quick marches and surprises. He must surround and astonish the foe, and take him at a disadvantage. To do this his own army must travel without baggage, so as to be able to move quickly, and must trust to finding all they needed for food and clothes in the country to which they went.

Napoleon knew that if the two armies of his enemies joined and attacked him together, they would be too strong for him. So he tried to keep them apart, and to fight first one and then the other. This he succeeded in doing. He led his soldiers with splendid skill. He beat every enemy who came against him, both in the plains of Italy and in the mountains of Austria. Nearly the whole of Italy was in his hands when at last peace was made.

First, a treaty, called the treaty of Leoben, from the name of the town in Austria where it was signed was agreed upon. Later came another, called the treaty of Campo Formio. By this treaty much land was added to France, and Napoleon made the first of those changes in the map of Europe for which he was soon to be famous.

Napoleon, in all his fighting in Italy, did not act merely as a commander and soldier. He acted more like a conqueror and ruler. It seemed as if he were not working for the Republic of France, but for himself. He did as he liked. "Do you suppose," he said, "that I triumph in Italy for the glory of the lawyers of the Directory? Do you suppose I mean to found a Republic? What an idea! The nation wants a chief, a chief covered with glory."

NAPOLEON AT LODI

He had covered himself with glory. His soldiers, whom he led with such splendid success, with such skill and daring, loved him.

They called him the "Little Corporal." This name they gave him after the crossing of the river Adda at the bridge of Lodi. The Austrians were on one side of the river, the French on the other. Shouting "Long live the Republic!" the French charged the bridge. But such a terrible fire met them that they wavered. Then Napoleon himself seized a standard and urged them onward. The bridge was passed. Right up to the enemy's guns they charged. The gunners died at their posts, but the Austrians were scattered, and fled in utter confusion, chased by the French, until darkness ended the flight and slaughter.

Napoleon himself called it "the terrible passage of Lodi," and it was after this battle that the French delighted with their clever leader called him the "Little Corporal," which for many a day was his name among his soldiers.

CHAPTER III

NAPOLEON IN EGYPT

After the treaty of Campo Formio was quite settled, Napoleon said good-bye to his army, and set out for Paris.

When he arrived, the people greeted him eagerly, and thronged to see him. They changed the name of the street in which he lived to Victory Street. But the rulers, the Directory, had begun to be afraid of this imperious soldier, who looked so small and delicate, and who had yet a will of iron, and seemed to hold the fate of nations in his hand. They were jealous of him too, for wherever he went, it was the conqueror of Italy who was cheered, not the rulers of France. And every soldier declared that it was high time to be done with lawyers, and make the "Little Corporal" king.

France and Britain were at this time bitter enemies, and the French were eager to conquer Britain. So Napoleon decided to carry out a plan which he had long thought of. That was to conquer Egypt, to found a colony there; and thus in some way injure Britain's trade with India and the East.

Egypt at this time was claimed by the Turks, and formed part of the Ottoman Empire. France and Turkey were at peace, but that made little difference to Napoleon.

The Directory agreed to Napoleon's plan for conquering Egypt. They were very anxious to get the better of Britain in some way, and they were not a little anxious to get rid of Napoleon, and keep him busy at something away from France.

For this expedition into Egypt Napoleon gathered together about twenty thousand of his finest soldiers and cleverest officers, and although the preparations were made with great secrecy, the British Government learned that something was going on. So Nelson was sent with some ships to watch the Mediterranean. But in May, when the French fleet was ready to sail, a great storm arose. It did such damage to the British ships that Nelson was obliged to put into a port in the island of Sardinia to repair them.

As soon as Napoleon knew that the way was clear, he gave orders to sail. On a beautiful May morning, just as the sun was rising, the great fleet sailed out on the waters of the Mediterranean. "Soldiers," said Napoleon to them as they set out, "you are one of the wings of the army of England. The eyes of all Europe are upon you. You are going to do more than you have ever done for the prosperity of your fatherland, for the good of man, and for your own glory." Besides speaking to them in this grand way, Napoleon promised each man that he should come home rich enough to buy six acres of land.

When Nelson found that Napoleon had left Toulon, he sailed up and down the Mediterranean looking for him, but he could not find him.

Meanwhile Napoleon reached Malta, took possession of the island, left a garrison of Frenchmen there, and sailed on his way to Egypt.

On the 30th of June, just as the sun was setting, Napoleon arrived at Alexandria. A storm was blowing, and such waves were beating upon the shore that it was dangerous to land. But seeing a strange sail in the distance, Napoleon would not wait. He feared that the British were at last upon his heels. "Fortune," he cried, "I ask but five hours. Will you deny them?"

And so, in the darkness and the storm, the troops were landed, but the waves were so fierce that many of the men were drowned.

Then through the night the French marched to Alexandria, and, wearied and hungry as they were, attacked it in the dawning of the day. The Turks and Arabs shut their gates and fought with all their might against this unexpected enemy. But the ancient walls could not stand the onslaught of Napoleon and his legions, and soon the flag of France was floating from the battlements.

In July Napoleon left Alexandria to march against Cairo. Many of his soldiers were old and tired men. They had endured the heat of Italy cheerfully, for there, although the sun was hot, they had marched through fertile lands well watered and pleasant. At the end of the day's march food and wine were always to be had. But now, day by day they marched over burning sand, under a brazen sky, through a land barren and empty, where neither man nor beast was to be seen, and where there was scarce a growing thing but thorny shrubs.

With feet burned and blistered, with parched tongues and cracked lips, blinded by the glare of the sun upon the sand, maddened by swarms of flies and insects, the march became a torture to the men. Gasping in the intolerable heat, they threw off their clothes, trying to find relief. Was this where the general had promised them six acres of land? they angrily demanded.

Even the officers could hardly bear the fiery torment. They pulled off their cockades and trod them in the sand and murmured of rebellion. Napoleon alone seemed cool and calm. He wore his heavy uniform, buttoned to the throat as usual, when the men were throwing away almost every garment. And when they were gasping and perspiring, he seemed as cool in body as in mind.

As the army wound along the weary way, many men, too worn out to keep up with the others, fell behind. Then out of the dust of the desert, through the glare of the dazzling sun, a company of fleet mounted Arabs would dash upon the stragglers. Muskets cracked, bright steel flashed, and the blood of Frenchmen stained the yellow desert sand.

For a fortnight the toilsome march dragged on through the seemingly endless wilds, until the men began to believe that there was no such place as Cairo. For the first time, they had lost faith in their leader.

Then, at last, one day over the unbroken waste of desert there rose enormous masses in straight lines and angles. They were the Pyramids.

Here the Mamelukes, as the Egyptian soldiers were called, awaited their enemy. Drawn out in glittering lines, with cannon pointed and camp entrenched, they waited.

Through a telescope Napoleon carefully examined the lines of the foe. He was a great general, but he noticed the smallest details. He now saw something which none of his officers had seen. The enemy's cannon were not on wheels. They were fixed, and could only be fired in one direction. That decided the day.

Napoleon drew up his men so that they should be out of range of the cannon. Then, pointing to the Pyramids as the battle began, "Soldiers," he cried, "forty centuries look down upon you."

And there in the sandy desert, under the burning sun, Mameluke and Frenchman fought. Flashing in the sunlight, the brilliant cavalcade came spurring on. Again and again it broke against the solid wall of glittering bayonets. The fight was fearful. When the Mamelukes could no longer shoot, they dashed their pistols in the faces of their enemies. When wounded, they crawled on the sand, hewing, hacking, and stabbing all that they could reach. But at last, scattered and thinned by the fearful charge of the French, the Mamelukes fled.

Many threw themselves into the Nile in the panic of flight. Many were cut down by the pursuing

French. Those who escaped carried to all parts of Egypt the fame and terror of Sultan Kebir, the King of Fire, as they called Napoleon.

BATTLE OF THE PYRAMIDS

Four days after the battle of the Pyramids, Napoleon entered Cairo. And here for some months he made his headquarters, ruling and commanding, fighting and punishing, making new laws for Egypt, much as a few months before he had done in Italy.

But meanwhile Napoleon's conquests in Egypt had been made useless, for the French fleet had been destroyed. Soon after the French soldiers had been landed, Nelson at last found the enemy he had been seeking so long, although Napoleon had escaped him. When the French and British fleets met, the battle of the Nile was fought, in which the French were utterly defeated. Of that battle you will read in the Life of Nelson.

When the news of the battle was brought to Napoleon he was filled with grief. Not only had the British, whom he had hoped to crush, been victorious once more, but by that victory he and his soldiers were cut off from France. Then the Turks, no longer having the French fleet to fear, declared war against France, and made ready an army to attack Napoleon in Egypt.

This army was expected to land in Syria, and Napoleon decided to meet it there. So once more the weary tramp through burning desert began.

Fighting and taking towns on the way the army at length reached Acre.

At this time a cruel ruler called Jessar Pasha, "the Butcher," lived there. Napoleon sent a message to this chief, hoping to win him to his side. But the Butcher cut off the messenger's head and threw his body into the sea in a sack.

So Napoleon began to besiege Acre. But now he had more than Turks against him. For Sir Sidney Smith, a British captain, was anchored in the bay, with two British ships, and he helped the Turks with men and guns.

For two months the siege went on. Napoleon had no battering-guns with which to break down the walls, for Sir Sidney Smith had seized his ships as they were coming from Alexandria with them. So he could make little impression. Then the plague broke out among his men, and at last, sorely against his will, Napoleon was forced to give up the siege and march back. In the darkness and silence of a May night the French army crept away. Thus ended Napoleon's dreams of power in the East. He had been beaten by the one enemy who was always to beat him—the British. For had no British ships been in the bay of Acre, the town might have fallen. "Had St. Jean d'Acre fallen, I would have changed the face of the world," said Napoleon.

The retreat from Acre was one long agony. The sun blazed down upon the weary and now disheartened soldiers, many of whom were wounded and ill. Those who were too ill to walk were borne in litters. But sometimes the men, tired of carrying their wounded comrades, and themselves scarcely able to drag along, would throw them down, and leave them to die by the wayside or fall into the hands of the terrible Turks.

Sometimes the thirsting troops would see in the distance a cool oasis, with waving palm trees and pools of sparkling water. Eagerly they would press forward, only to find a few moments later that what they had seen was a mirage, a deceitful picture of the desert.

Sometimes, when they did find water, it was so foul or salt that their thirst was made worse rather than better. And all the way they were beset by pursuing Turks and wild desert Arabs, so that many more died on the march than in the battle. But at last their miseries were ended, and the worn-out army reached Cairo again.

Here Napoleon set himself once more to the ruling of Egypt, and by a great victory over the Turks at Aboukir Bay he blotted out the memory of his defeat at Acre.

All during the time of the Syrian campaign Napoleon had had no news of France. Now some old newspapers came into his hands. From them he learned that things were indeed going ill at home. Italy was lost, and all his great conquests were wiped out as if they had never been.

"The fools have lost Italy," he exclaimed. "All the fruits of my victories have disappeared. I must leave Egypt."

But he had no ships in which to carry his army home. So he resolved to go alone, taking only about five hundred men with him, and leaving one of his generals in charge of the campaign, which from the beginning had been utterly useless.

Napoleon made all his preparations with great secrecy; he dared not tell his soldiers that he was going to desert them. One dark August night, under the pale light of the twinkling stars, as silently as possible the company rode down to the harbour of Alexandria. Quickly and stealthily the men went on board two waiting vessels which instantly set sail for home.

CHAPTER IV

NAPOLEON AS CONSUL

When Napoleon arrived in France, the people greeted him more joyfully than ever. They were weary of the rule of the Directory, and longed for a change. Napoleon had never meant to be a soldier and conqueror only; he meant to be a ruler too. He soon saw his chance and took it.

He had been made commander of all the troops round Paris, and now one day he appeared at the head of his soldiers in the courtyard of the palace in which the French Assembly, or Parliament, sat. Amid a fearful noise of shouts, beating of drums, and tramp of feet, the Assembly was turned out at the point of the bayonet. That night Napoleon slept in the palace of the Luxembourg, with the title of Consul of France.

There were three other consuls. But the others were a mere pretence. Napoleon was the true ruler.

Napoleon returned from Egypt in October and by the middle of December he was First Consul. Then for the next few months he gave himself up to ruling. Under his firm hand France, which had been torn and tossed in wild unrest for eight years, now seemed to find a little calm.

But all around the borders of France there was war still. Austria and Britain were her chief enemies. With Britain, at this time, Napoleon would have been glad to make peace, could he have done so on his own terms. Austria he meant to crush, and to crush in such a way as would make Europe ring with the name of Bonaparte. He meant to do great deeds at which the world would stare and wonder. He meant to have peace too, but peace after victory.

The army of Italy was still fighting under a brave general called Massena. But now he was shut up in Genoa, a British fleet bombarding him from the sea, and an Austrian army surrounding him on land. Food was growing scarce, and his men were but worn-out skeletons. The Austrians believed that they should very soon beat him, and then they would be able to march into France.

Napoleon now gathered an army, called the Reserve, with which, he gave out, he was going to march to the help of Massena. But the Austrians laughed at the Reserve army, for it was made up of ill-fed, half-clothed, raw recruits. Napoleon went to Dijon to review these new recruits. But he stayed there only two hours and was soon speeding on his way to Geneva.

For three months Napoleon had been silently and secretly gathering troops which by different ways had been sent towards Switzerland. There, too, engineers had been sent to examine the passes through the Alps. Now everything was ready, and the great commander also went speeding to the land of snow mountains.

When Napoleon arrived at Geneva he gathered his engineers around him and began to study the map of the Alps.

"Is it possible to pass?" he asked.

"It is barely possible," said an engineer.

"Very well," replied Napoleon; "let us be going."

Then Napoleon began one of his most famous marches. He crossed the Alps, and, while the enemy awaited him in front, he appeared suddenly behind them.

The army was divided into four, each part going by a different way. The ways through the mountains are called passes. The passes which Napoleon now chose were the Great St. Bernard, the Little St. Bernard, the Mont Cenis, and the St. Gotthard.

Napoleon himself went by the Great St. Bernard.

It was a tremendous march, for in places there was not even a track, and the men had to stumble as best they could over rough, broken, stony ground. Up and up they struggled, for a pass is only comparatively low; that is, low when compared with the huge mountains near. The Great St. Bernard pass is more than eight thousand feet above sea-level. It was hard enough for men laden with knapsack and gun to toil upwards, but to drag heavy cannon up was still harder. The path was so terrible that it was found to be quite impossible to bring them up on their carriages. No wheels could pass over the grounds so each cannon was taken from its carriage, and was put into the trunk of a tree, which had been hollowed out to fit it. A hundred men were then harnessed to each tree-trunk, and so the cannon were dragged over snow and ice, along narrow, giddy paths where only the chamois or the goat herd had left a track. The carriages were taken to pieces, the wheels were slung on poles and carried on men's shoulders.

Food for the army had to be carried too. This was laden on mules. They were sure-footed, hardy beasts accustomed to the wild mountain-sides, and so could carry weight even over the rough path. But with the cavalry horses it was different. The men dismounted, and each man led his horse as best he could.

Thus for five days an endless stream of men and horses passed among the silent hills, churning the white snow into a brown morass, filling the still air with the hum of voices and the clank and gangle of steel, awaking the echoes with the sound of drum and trumpet. On and on went the men, slipping, sliding, panting, breathless, hardly daring to pause in places lest those behind should be thrown into confusion, stumbling knee-deep into snowdrifts, clambering round boulders, but always upward and upward. At last they reached the summit of the pass.

Here is the Hospice of St Bernard, founded by St. Bernard de Menthon nearly a thousand years ago. And here all the year round live the good monks of St. Bernard, ever ready to aid travellers.

When the wearied soldiers reached the top of the pass the good monks gave them a meal of bread and wine and cheese, and then the long descent began. For the horses and mules this was almost more difficult than the ascent. But sliding and stumbling they at last got over the worst of the road with no serious accident.

But a new difficulty now arose. Fort Bard had to be passed. This was only a little fort held by four hundred Austrians, but, perched upon a rock, it commanded the tiny town through which the road lay, and the whole pass, which here is not more than fifty yards wide.

For some time the French tried in vain to take the fort. Then at length they discovered a narrow goat-track leading round it, and out of gun-shot. By this, one by one, the infantry passed, but it was impossible to take the artillery that way. So in the dead of night the artillery-men entered the village. They spread chaff and straw upon the street, and having muffled every belt or buckle that might clatter or jingle, they drew the cannon through the town, almost under the noses of the unsuspecting Austrians.

Then, the last difficulty being passed, the French poured like an avalanche down upon the plain of Italy.

The news of Napoleon's wonderful march soon reached the famished garrison of Genoa, and the thought that help was near renewed their sinking courage. But day after day passed, and no rescuing French army appeared before the walls. Still they hoped on, sick at heart and weary. But at length the last spark of hope died, and brave Massena gave in. They had absolutely nothing left to eat but knapsacks and shoes, grass and roots.

"No terms are too good for you," said Lord Keith, the British commander. So the French were allowed to march out with all the honours of war.

Meanwhile Napoleon was passing through Italy in a kind of triumph. It did not suit his plans to relieve Genoa, so he left the garrison to starve, while he prepared for a great battle in which all was to be won or lost.

And so at last French and Austrian met again upon the field of Marengo, a little village not far from the town of Alessandria.

At daybreak on the 14th of June the fight began. It was a fierce and terrible battle. The Austrians numbered nearly twice as many as the French. At one time the French fled from the field, crying, "All is lost." Again they rallied, but step by step they were driven backward, and at last fled once more. The Austrian leader was an old man of over eighty. He was weary of long fighting, and about three o'clock in the afternoon, believing the victory won, he left the field.

But at this moment a French officer who had been at some distance rode up, with fresh troops. "I fear it is a battle lost," he said to Napoleon.

"I think it is a battle won," replied he. And rallying his men, and ordering a sudden charge of cavalry, he turned defeat into victory. Soon it was the Austrians who were fleeing from the field in utter rout.

So completely crushed was the Austrian army that next day their leader sent a flag of truce to Napoleon, begging for peace. And by the treaty which followed all Northern Italy was given up almost as it had been at the treaty of Campo Formio. Thus at one blow was Italy reconquered.

Having thus startled the world, and covered his name with glory, Napoleon returned to Paris. He had been gone less than two months. All along the way people crowded to cheer him as he passed. In Paris the houses were lit up night after night in his honour. For hours together crowds would stand round his palace hoping to catch a glimpse of the conqueror of the Alps, of the victor of Marengo. Napoleon was delighted with all the fame he had won. "A few more events like this campaign, and I shall perhaps go down to posterity," he cried.

CHAPTER V

NAPOLEON AS EMPEROR

France now made peace with all Europe, and for the next few years Napoleon ruled France quietly. These few years are really the best part of all his life. In them he did many good things for his country. And these lasted when all his great conquests faded, and his vast Empire crumbled into pieces.

Gradually his power grew greater and greater. From being Consul for ten years he was made Consul for life. Then he was asked to take the title of Emperor, and on the 18th of May 1804 he was proclaimed Emperor of the French.

The "little corporal" had come far. He who, a few years before, had wandered almost penniless among the streets of Paris, was now the greatest man in all the land. He seemed to have reached the very highest power that man could hope for, and he was not yet thirty-five years old.

But although Napoleon had been proclaimed Emperor, and accepted by the people of France, he had not yet been crowned. Now he felt that to be crowned and anointed by the Pope would make his throne more sure. So he sent a friend to Rome, to ask the Pope to come to crown him.

Pope Pius VII. did not want to crown Napoleon, and acknowledge him as the rightful ruler of France. But he saw that nearly all the other rulers of Europe had acknowledged him, and he thought it better to do so too, as perhaps he might in that way win something good for the Church. So he consented to come to Paris to crown the Emperor.

The Pope, as head of the Church, had been treated with fear and reverence by the proudest of kings in all ages and in all countries. They had knelt to him as to one greater than themselves. But Napoleon had grown so proud that he could not bear the thought of kneeling to any one. So, although he very well knew the hour at which the Pope might be expected to arrive, he arranged to meet him as if by accident while out hunting.

As the Pope's coach drove along the road leading to the palace of Fontainebleau which had been prepared for him, he met the Emperor, booted and spurred, and riding upon a horse.

The Emperor got off his horse, and the Pope, in his beautiful robes and white silk shoes, left his coach, and walked a few steps along the muddy road to greet him.

The young Emperor and the old Pope embraced each other, then the servants, having received their orders before, drove the coach up between them. The footmen opened both doors at once, and as the Pope stepped in at one side the Emperor stepped in

NAPOLEON AND THE POPE

at the other, so neither went in before the other. But Napoleon took care that he had the seat of honour, on the right side. Thus Pope and Emperor drove to Fontainebleau.

There were a great many preparations for the coronation to be made, for Napoleon meant it to be a very fine affair. But at last; everything was ready, and on the 2nd of December the coronation took place. The day was cold and bleak, but the streets of Paris were lined with people, eager to see the Emperor and Empress as they drove in their gilded carriage to the Church of Notre Dame.

The church was thronged with fair ladies and splendid men glittering with jewels and lace, and as the Emperor entered, wearing upon his head a wreath of golden bay leaves like a Cæsar, the archways of the dim old church rang and rang again with shouts, "Long live the Emperor! Long live the Emperor!"

The notes of the organ rolled, the voices of the choir rose and fell in chant and hymn. But as the long ceremony went on, Napoleon yawned and fidgeted. To him there was nothing sacred or solemn in the service. The grand display added something to his pomp and glory; that was all.

At last the Pope with trembling hands lifted the crown to place it upon the young Emperor's head. But Napoleon, seizing it out of the Pope's hand, himself placed it upon his own head, took it off, placed it for a moment on the head of the Empress, and then returned it to the cushion upon which it had rested.

Again the organ pealed, and the exultant words of the "Te Deum" rang out through the church.

The Emperor was crowned.

A few months after the coronation at Notre Dame, Napoleon went to Italy. Here, in the great cathedral at Milan, he again crowned himself. This time the title he took was King of Italy, and this time the Pope sternly refused to have anything to do with it. At Paris he had received only empty promises and insults as his reward, and he now knew that he had nothing to hope from the new Emperor.

But while Napoleon was placing crowns upon his own head, the rulers of Europe were again joining against him. For they saw that the Emperor's power, and desire for still more power, were becoming so great that none of their crowns were safe.

Sweden, Russia, and Austria joined the alliance. But, on the other hand, Spain and Britain, having quarrelled, Spain joined with France against the others. Once more Europe was ablaze with war. Upon the Rhine, in Tyrol, in Italy, there was noise of battle.

The Czar of Russia gathered a great army and sent it to join the Austrians. When they joined, it was intended that both armies should march together into France.

But the Austrians began to fight before the Russians joined them. Napoleon did not wait for France to be invaded. He marched into Germany to meet his enemies. And long before the Russians could arrive to help them, the Austrians were shut up in the town of Ulm.

The Austrian leader, Mack, was not cowardly, but he was stupid and unlucky. And although there was plenty of food within the walls, Mack weakly gave in after six days' siege.

In Tyrol, in Italy, everywhere that the French and Austrians met, the Austrians were defeated, until at last a flying remnant of Mack's once splendid army took refuge in the mountains of Tyrol. There was nothing now to hinder Napoleon from marching on to Vienna, the beautiful capital of Austria.

And the Emperor Francis, knowing that Vienna could not stand a siege more than a few days, made up his mind to leave the town. So on the 13th of November, less than a month after the taking of Ulm, the French entered the Austrian capital.

While Napoleon was at Vienna, living in the Emperor's beautiful palace of Schönbrunn, bad tidings came to him. He heard that the French and Spanish fleets had been utterly destroyed in the battle of Trafalgar.

"I cannot be everywhere," cried he angrily, when he heard the news.

That the French had again been defeated by sea made the Emperor more eager to win fresh fame by land. The Austrian army was shattered, but the Russians were still to beat. So from Vienna Napoleon marched out to meet them. Upon the plain of Austerlitz, not far from the town of Brunn, a great battle was fought. It has been called "the battle of the three Emperors," for there were three Emperors present—the Emperor of Germany (the Holy Roman Empire), the Emperor of Russia, and the Emperor of the French.

The morning of the 2nd December dawned cold and bleak. A thick white fog shrouded the land. But with the first streak of day both camps were astir. Through the white dimness came muffled sounds, and ghostly figures loomed and passed. Then suddenly the fog lifted; and the sun shone out in golden splendour. The French soldiers greeted it with a shout. It seemed to them as if it rose to do honour to their own Emperor, for it was the anniversary of his coronation day. "The sun of Austerlitz has risen," cried Napoleon in exultation.

In the fog the two armies had moved close to each, and now the fight began. It was a terrible battle, and raged all the short winter's day. "It was absolute butchery," says one who fought there. "We fought man to man."

For a time it seemed uncertain who should win, but when the night fell the Russians and Austrians were flying from the field. Many lay there dead, and twenty thousand were prisoners.

Thus once more Napoleon had triumphed. And now Austria made peace with France, and the Russians marched away to their own land. This peace was called the treaty of Pressburg, from the name of the town at which it was signed.

By this treaty the map of Europe was again changed and still more lands came under Napoleon's rule. Some of these lands he gave to his relations. For Napoleon had made up his mind not only to be great himself, but to make his whole family great. "I can no longer have shabby relatives," he said. "Those who will not rise with me shall no longer be of my family. I am going to make a family of kings."

So he made his brother Joseph King of Naples. His brother Louis, who had married Josephine's daughter Hortense, was made King of Holland. General Murat, who had married Napoleon's sister Caroline, was made Archduke of Berg. He made Eugène Beauharnais marry the daughter of the King of Bavaria, and a little later he made his brother Jerome marry the daughter of the King of Würtemberg. In every way Napoleon tried to make his family great, and so surround himself with splendour.

CHAPTER VI

NAPOLEON AND PRUSSIA

All this time Prussia, the greatest of the German states, had held aloof. The King was very unwilling to plunge his people into war. So he tried to be neutral and keep the peace. Prussia had a large and, it was thought, well-drilled army, and as long as Napoleon had the Russians and the Austrians to fight, he was not sorry, perhaps, that Prussia should keep peace. He even tried to bribe the King not to fight by offering to give him the Electorate of Hanover. The Electorate of Hanover was of course not his to give. It belonged to the King of Britain.

But now, having got rid of the Russians and the Austrians, Napoleon was very insulting to the King of Prussia. Whether he really meant to insult him, and so drive him to war, or whether he was only bent on having his own way, without caring how he hurt others, does not matter. A new war, this time between France and Prussia, soon began.

Britain, Russia, and Austria would all have helped Prussia, but King Frederick William, after having held back for so long, now rushed into war before his own plans or those of the allies were ready.

Although Prussia had a great army, many of the officers were old, and the country had been so long at peace that they had forgotten the best ways of fighting.

Napoleon, on the other hand, was always fighting, always watchful, always ready. So just as he had quickly marched against the Austrians, before the Russians had time to come to help them, now he marched against the Prussians.

It was near Jena that the great battle of the campaign was fought.

Like the dawn of Austerlitz, the dawn of Jena was shrouded in mist. Not until ten o'clock did the thick clouds roll away and the warm October sun shine out. Then, and not till then, did the Prussian leader see that he had to fight, not a small part of the French army, as he had thought, but more than eighty-three thousand men, under the great Emperor himself. He himself had scarcely more than half that number.

Once more the battle raged, and once more it ended in a great victory for Napoleon, and the Prussians were scattered in fearful rout.

On the same day, and at the same time, another battle was fought. This was at Auerstadt, about fifteen miles away. It was fought by the other half of the Prussian army, against the French under General Davoust.

King Frederick William was with this army, and at Auerstadt the Prussians far outnumbered the French. But still the result was the same, and the French won the day. The fleeing remnants of both armies met, and mingled, and fled to the nearest fortresses for safety. Thus in one day the great army of Prussia was crushed.

Masses of French soldiers now poured into Prussia, and the Prussian fortresses fell one after the other into their hands. Whether the garrisons were overcome with fear at Napoleon's great name, or whether some of them betrayed their country, for one reason or another the fortresses made little resistance, but gave in quickly, and the conqueror marched in triumph to Berlin.

Crushed and dispirited, the King of Prussia tried to make peace. But Napoleon asked too much—his terms were too hard. He demanded the whole of Prussia, as far as the Vistula. Crushed though he was, the King was not ready to yield as much as that. The Russians, too, were now marching to help him. So the war went on, and it was now carried into Poland.

The march through Poland was terrible. As a general rule, it had been the custom to stop fighting during winter, and begin again in the spring. But Napoleon bound himself by no such rules. So, through rain, sleet, and snow, over roads knee-deep in mud, the army moved on. The sufferings of the soldiers were great. Their boots and clothes were worn out, and not nearly warm enough. For the winter so far north is much colder than in France. Food was hard to get, no bread was to be had, the water was muddy and bad, the houses were mere hovels, where men, cows, and pigs all lived together. "And this is what the Poles have the impudence to call a country," said the French soldiers in disgust. "In Poland we have found a fifth element," said Napoleon; "it is mud."

Thus, fighting and marching, in cold, wet, and hunger, the army passed the Vistula.

Now at last, seeing that his men were utterly worn out, Napoleon consented to rest. He took up his headquarters at Warsaw, the capital of the province, while the army found quarters in the little villages along the banks of the Vistula.

Napoleon's weary soldiers were, however, only allowed about a month's rest. For the Russians, more used to the bitter cold than the French, began to make ready for battle as soon as the swamps and marshes, hardened by frost, made it once more possible for horses and cannon to pass.

At a little place called Preuss Eylau, not far from Königsberg, a terrible battle took place. The day was dark and lowering. Heavy clouds covered the grey sky, a bitter wind drove the frozen snow, stinging the faces of the hungry, ill-fed men, who the night before had supped on nothing but potatoes.

Yet in the midst of all this misery and discomfort both sides fought with a terrible, brutal courage. "The Russians fought like bulls," said the French. Their famous Cossack horsemen charged, and wheeled, and charged again. Cannon roared, muskets cracked and rattled. And amid the screams and horrid clangour of battle, the silent white snow whirled and fell, to be trampled and reddened with the blood of fifty thousand men. At last the short winter's day was over, and darkness covered the dreadful field, which in the morning had lain so white and unstained.

Both sides claimed the victory. But indeed it was only a useless slaughter. "What a massacre!" cried a French officer, as next day he rode across the field. "What a massacre, and without result!"

After the battle of Preuss Eylau both armies were so shattered that until the winter passed there was little more fighting. Napoleon even tried to make peace with King Frederick William, offering him this time much better terms than before. But the King answered that he could only make a peace which would include the Czar of Russia; so no peace was made.

With the coming of summer, the struggle began once more. After some fierce fighting, the war came to an end with a battle fought near the little town of Friedland.

From dawn to dark the battle lasted. The Russians fought fiercely and well. But Napoleon, as he rode about among his cheering, saluting men, cried again and again, "To-day is a lucky day. It is the anniversary of Marengo." So, roused by the memory of that great fight, the French fought with double courage. At last the Russian army, broken and dismayed, fled across the Pregel, followed closely by the pursuing French. Then, driven still at the sword's point, day by day they fled, in utter rout, until they passed the Niemen. Behind this broad river they found shelter from their foes.

Upon the one bank lay the remains of the Russian army, upon the other the French. And now that his army was shattered, the Czar sought for peace. And Napoleon, for many reasons, was ready to listen.

In the middle of the Niemen, opposite the town of Tilsit, a gaily-decorated and curtained raft was moored. Over it floated the eagle of France and the eagle of Russia. Here the two Emperors met and embraced, like brothers rather than enemies. They then went within the curtains and talked for a long time, no one being near to hear what was said. But when they came out again they seemed more friendly than before.

After this meeting the town of Tilsit, which is in Prussia, but only a few miles from the Russian frontier, was declared neutral, and both Emperors went to live there, and held their courts each in a different part of the town.

Now, instead of the horror of war, the town was full of gaiety. There were riding parties, dinners, and balls. And the Emperors, who a few days before had been bitter enemies, seemed to have become the best of friends.

The Emperor of Russia was young and handsome. He was full of splendid dreams, and eager to be great. Napoleon too was young—he was only thirty-seven, and already he was the greatest conqueror, soldier, and statesman in the world.

Napoleon was often fierce, hard, and cruel; but when he chose he could seem friendly and lovable. He conquered men and women as he conquered peoples. Now he won the heart of the young Czar. "I never had more prejudices against any one than against him," he said; "but after three-quarters of an hour of talk they all vanished as a dream. Would that I had seen him sooner."

The poor beaten King of Prussia was asked also to come to Tilsit. But Napoleon, who treated the Czar so kindly, treated the King very coldly. He and his Queen, who came with him, were not allowed to live in Tilsit. They had to put up with a little mill-house outside the town. Napoleon tried in many ways to make the Prussian King and Queen feel that they were crushed and beaten enemies. It was only out of friendship to the Czar, he said, that the King had been asked to Tilsit at all. And in the drawing up of the treaty no pity for him was shown. By it Frederick William lost half his states.

CHAPTER VII

NAPOLEON IN SPAIN

Besides fighting with Britain Napoleon tried to conquer our islands by ruining our trade. He forbade all the countries on the Continent to trade with Britain.

But in spite of Napoleon's orders Portugal went on trading with Britain. Now, soon after Napoleon returned from Tilsit he sent a message to the Prince Regent of Portugal, telling him that he must stop trading with Britain, must seize all British goods and property in Portugal, and declare war with Britain. If he did not do all this, Napoleon threatened that he would declare war with Portugal.

Portugal is only a little country, quite unable to stand against such a powerful conqueror as Napoleon. So the Prince Regent agreed to all that was asked, except the seizing of British goods. That he would not do. Then Napoleon prepared to fight.

France at this time had hardly any navy. Napoleon had not enough ships in which to send his troops by sea. To make war on Portugal he had to pass through Spain. So he now made a secret treaty with the King of Spain by which his troops were to be allowed

54

to pass through that country. And when by the help of Spanish soldiers he had conquered Portugal, he promised to divide it with Spain.

The kingdom of Portugal was at this time ruled by a Regent. The Queen, Maria I., was mad, and her son, Prince John, ruled for her. Now when the Regent heard that Napoleon was gathering an army to fight him, he made up his mind to leave the war to Britain, and take his poor, mad mother away to Brazil, which was then a Portuguese colony. So, one wet and cold November morning the Queen and Prince and many of the nobles set sail, leaving a sad and mourning people behind.

Meanwhile Napoleon had gathered a large army at Bayonne, a strongly-fortified town close to the Pyrenees, but on the French side of them. This army, under Marshal Junot, now came marching quickly through Spain to Lisbon, the capital of Portugal. They crossed the Pyrenees, which, next to the Alps, are the highest mountains in Europe. Over the wind-swept plain they came, across rivers, down rugged valleys, by muddy tracks which could scarcely be called roads. The men grew weary, but Junot urged them onward. The land was barren and bare, and they had often hardly enough to eat. For, as was usual with Napoleon's armies, they carried no supplies with them, but trusted to finding what they needed in the land they passed through. "I will not have the march kept back because of supplies," said the Emperor. "Twenty thousand men can find food anywhere, even in a desert." Most of the soldiers in this army were mere boys, raw recruits, unused to such hardships. Many of them dropped out of the ranks, overcome with weariness, and were left by the wayside to die.

At last, little more than a month after they had set out from Bayonne, they arrived, footsore, hungry, and ragged, at Lisbon, too late. The ship carrying the Queen and Prince was already far out to sea.

The royal family had escaped, but the French took possession of the country. There was little fighting. Had there been in the Portuguese army even a handful of bold and resolute men, it might have gone ill with Junot's raw and worn-out soldiers. But there were none such.

Everywhere the French pulled down the royal arms of Portugal, and set those of Napoleon up. Many of the Portuguese soldiers were sent away to France, so that they might not have a chance of fighting for their country even if a leader should appear. The Portuguese people were made to pay great sums of money to the conqueror, who declared that the House of Braganza—that is, the royal house of Portugal—had ceased to reign.

And while all this was happening, French troops kept on pouring into Spain, in far greater numbers than were needed to conquer little Portugal.

"Write descriptions of all the provinces through which you pass," said Napoleon, as he sent them away. "Describe the roads and the nature of the land. Send me sketches, that I may see the distance of the villages, the nature of the country, and the resources of the land." All this was not necessary if he merely intended to pass through the land to reach Portugal. No, he had another design, far greater than the conquest of Portugal, in his mind.

Spain at this time was badly ruled. The King, Charles IV., was old and foolish. All the power was in the hands of the Queen, who was not a good woman, and of Manuel Godoy, her favourite. He was not a good man, but he had been given the beautiful name of the Prince of Peace, because at one time he had helped to make a peace with France.

The King's eldest son, Ferdinand, hated Godoy, and quarrelled with him. So the court of Spain was full of strife. Now both sides appealed to Napoleon for help. It was rather like mice putting their heads into a cat's mouth. The King and Queen began to think so, and they decided to run away, as the Queen and Prince of Portugal had done, and take refuge from all their troubles in America.

But when the people found out what they meant to do, they were very angry, and broke out into a riot. They burst into Godoy's palace in search of the man they hated. They could not find him, so they wreaked their vengeance on the beautiful furniture and pictures, leaving the palace a waste of splinters and rags. Meanwhile, he, trembling in fear, was hiding in a roll of matting in the attic.

There for two days he remained, until at last, driven by hunger, he crept out. He hoped to escape unseen, but at once he was seized, and would have been torn to pieces by the angry mob, had not Prince Ferdinand begged for his life.

Now the weak old King of Spain, trembling for the life of his friend, the Prince of Peace, decided to give up the throne to his son Ferdinand. He hoped in this way to quiet the riot. But the people, when they heard the news, went mad with joy, and to show it, they burned and sacked the houses belonging to Godoy, his friends, and relatives, while they proclaimed Ferdinand King with shouting and cheering.

But their joy was short-lived. Almost at once the old King began to be sorry that he had given up the crown, and wanted it back again. And meanwhile French troops were closing in round Madrid.

Soon it became known that Napoleon himself was coming. And hearing that his father and mother were going to meet the Emperor, Ferdinand resolved to go too, and lay his case before him. The people were very unwilling that he should go, for they felt sure that some evil would befall their young King. At one place, as he travelled through the land, they cut the traces of his horses, thinking to make him give up his intention. But he went on.

As there was still no sign of Napoleon when Ferdinand reached the border, he crossed into France, and met him at Bayonne.

There too came the old King, the Queen, and Manuel Godoy. Beyond their own borders, surrounded by French soldiers, they were Napoleon's prisoners. They had of free will, it seemed, walked into the trap.

And now Napoleon told them that it was useless to quarrel about who should be King of Spain, as he wanted the throne for one of his own family. "The House of Bourbon has ceased to reign," he said, in his usual grand way.

What could the poor Spanish Kings do? The whole country was in the hands of the French, and they themselves prisoners in a foreign land. So at the bidding of Napoleon they signed away the crown and throne of Spain.

Without striking a blow, Napoleon had added two more kingdoms to his conquests; and with Spain went all her rich colonies. But it had been done by base treachery. Even he himself long after said, "The whole thing wears an ugly look since I have fallen."

Napoleon now made his brother Joseph King of Spain. But the people of Spain would have no Bonaparte to reign over them. The Spaniards, though the most polite and courteous of men, are idle and indolent, seldom showing any energy. But now they were thoroughly roused. To a man they rebelled. From every town and village they flocked, ready to fight for their freedom and their King.

Meanwhile the new King Joseph, guarded by French troops, came to live in the capital.

The Spaniards received him in sullen silence. And as Joseph looked at the dark faces which surrounded him, he felt that he had not a friend among them.

Everywhere there was fighting. Yet so sure was Napoleon that now everything would go on in Spain just as he wished, that he left Bayonne, and set out on a tour through some of the French towns.

But even as Napoleon started, messengers were speeding northward, with the news that General Dupont and all his men had surrendered to the Spaniards.

Napoleon was furiously angry. "Could I have expected that from Dupont!" he cried. "A man I loved! He had no other way to save his soldiers? Better, far better, to have died with arms in their hands. You can always supply the place of soldiers. Honour alone, once lost, can never be regained."

Everywhere all through Spain battles were fought, towns were besieged. One of the most famous sieges was that of Saragossa. The fortifications were poor; but the hearts of the people were stout. Day by day they held out, the women fighting beside the men. One woman, named Maria Augustin, became famous, and was called "the Maid of Saragossa." She fought beside her lover, helping him to fire the cannon of which he was in charge, and when he fell dead, she still went on fighting and worked the cannon herself.

Hunger and disease fought against the brave defenders. Still they held out. But the French at last gained possession of a convent which was almost within the walls. Their leader then sent a summons, to the town. It was short and sharp. "Headquarters, St. Engracia. Surrender," was all it said.

The reply was as sharp. "Headquarters, Saragossa. War to the knife."

The Maid of Saragossa

At last, hearing of the defeat at Bailen, where Dupont and all his men had laid down their arms to the Spaniards, the French gave up the siege of Saragossa and marched away, "Foil'd by a woman's hand, before a battered wall."

Afterwards, when the war of liberation was over, Maria Augustin received medals, as did other soldiers, in reward for her bravery, and her portrait was bought by people all over Europe. It was long ere the name of the Maid of Saragossa was forgotten.

But now Spain was not left to fight her war of liberation unaided. Britain had been at war with Spain. In the battle of Trafalgar the fleet of Spain had been destroyed with that of France. "But the kingdom thus nobly struggling against the usurpation and tyranny of France can no longer be considered as the enemy of Great Britain," said King George. "It is recognised by me as a natural friend and ally."

So British troops were sent to help the Spaniards in their struggle. And thus began for us the war which we call the Peninsular War.

It will be impossible to follow all this war. The story of it belongs to another place, especially as Napoleon himself was very little with his soldiers in Spain. For even while this great struggle was going on he began another war with Austria. Indeed it was not only the Austrians who now fought. In Tyrol the peasants had risen under a brave leader called Hofer. In Germany, in Poland, in Italy, everywhere, the people rose. In many places they won battles. But after all, where Napoleon led, there was the heart of the fight. And he was everywhere victorious.

It was near the village of Wagram that the deciding battle of the war took place. The Austrians fought with splendid courage, and when night came, of the fifty thousand who lay dead, nearly as many were French as Austrian. It was one of the fiercest battles ever fought, and to Napoleon it counted barely a victory.

Yet for the Emperor of Austria it was enough. He was not made of the stern stuff of heroes and patriots. Once more he yielded. And on the 14th of October the treaty of Schönbrunn, so called from the name of the beautiful palace in Vienna where Napoleon was living, was signed.

By this treaty Austria lost still more land. Napoleon took for France the lands lying round the Adriatic. Parts of Upper Austria, Galicia, and Bohemia were given to Napoleon's vassal kings to reward them for having helped him. For it must be remembered that Napoleon's great armies were not made up only of Frenchmen, but of men from every country which he had conquered, or over whose ruler he held sway.

After the treaty of Schönbrunn was signed, Napoleon returned to Paris.

And now one of the strangest things in his life happened. You remember that long ago, when the Emperor was a poor soldier, he had married a beautiful lady, called Josephine de Beauharnais. He had loved her very much. "To live for Josephine—that is the history of my life," he had written then. "I prize honour since you prize it; I prize victory since it pleases you."

Now glory, if not honour, was heaped upon him. He had piled victory upon victory, but he forgot what he had written as a young and eager boy. He put away his beautiful wife, and married the Duchess Marie Louise, the daughter of his late enemy the Emperor of Austria.

One reason why Napoleon did this was that his pride had grown with his power. He still loved Josephine, but he longed to have a great lady for his wife—a princess, the daughter of a long line of kings, to be the mother of his children.

Marie Louise was little more than a girl. She had hated Napoleon, and once when she heard that he had been defeated, she said that she was glad, and hoped that it would happen again. Now she came to be his wife, because her father told her, perhaps, that this marriage would help to bring peace and freedom to her country. So she became the Empress Marie Louise.

CHAPTER VIII

NAPOLEON IN RUSSIA

On the 10th of March 1811 a little son was born to Napoleon, who at once gave him the title of King of Rome. With a son to follow him upon the throne, Napoleon seemed to be at the very height of his glory. "Now begins the finest epoch of my reign," he said. At forty-one he seemed to have the world at his feet. Really his downfall had begun.

The people of Russia had found Napoleon's orders not to trade with Britain very hard, and the Czar became less and less inclined to make his people keep them. As more and more British goods were allowed to pass into Russia, Napoleon grew more and more angry. There were other reasons for quarrelling, and at last war broke out between the two rival Emperors, who at Tilsit had sworn to be friends.

Napoleon decided utterly to crush his great rival, and to force all Europe over which he had control to help him.

So he gathered a mighty army, six hundred thousand strong. From all the states of Germany, from Prussia, Austria, Holland, Belgium, Italy, Poland,

Switzerland, even from Spain and Portugal, soldiers came to swell the host which poured across the Niemen in three great bodies.

But it was a barren, empty country into which they passed. No enemy even awaited them; only a few horsemen watched as they came. "Why do you come into Russia?" they asked.

"To conquer you," was the reply, and the horsemen galloped silently away, and disappeared into the forests beyond.

With the French army came an enormous baggage train. But Napoleon had so long used his armies to believe that they would find all they needed in the countries they invaded, that this part of the army was very badly managed. Almost at once the soldiers began to suffer from hunger.

As Napoleon advanced into the country, the Russians retreated.

Day after day along dusty, sandy roads, past burned and deserted villages and towns, through dreary, silent, barren plains, the retreat and chase went on. The air was hot and close, the sun shone pitilessly. The men marched wearily, for they were parched with thirst and always hungry. They had little to eat, except what they could find by scouring the country far and wide.

There was much fierce fighting by the way. One of these fights, called the battle of Borodino, is the deadliest battle of all Napoleon's wars, and it is known as "the generals' battle," for twenty-two Russian and eighteen French generals were among the slain.

At last one beautiful autumn morning, about a week after the battle of Borodino, Napoleon and his army caught the first sight of Moscow, from the top of a little hill called the Hill of Salvation, which overlooks it.

"Moscow! Moscow!" The cry ran down the lines. To the weary men Moscow was the haven of rest towards which they had been struggling those hundreds and hundreds of dreary miles. Now it lay before them, glittering white in the sunshine, with its many-coloured roofs, gilded domes, spires, and turrets. "The Asiatic town of countless churches, Moscow the Holy," cried Napoleon, reining in his horse. "There at last is the famous town. It was time!"

But when Napoleon and his army marched through the streets, they were silent and deserted. Here and there a timid or scowling face might be seen. But the streets echoed with a hollow sound, and the empty houses stared down upon the soldiers with closed shutters, like sightless eyes.

For days every one who could leave the city had been hurrying away, and the roads had been full of a constant stream of clattering carriages and rumbling carts laden with people and their goods. The night before Napoleon had entered, the troops also had gone. All night long the steady tramp, tramp, had sounded through the streets. The great military stores had been burned or destroyed, the prisons opened, and the prisoners set free, the fire-engines made useless, and the great city, mostly built of wood, left to the mercy of the rabble and the foe.

Scarcely two hours after the last soldier had gone, the French arrived. And when they found the city silent and empty, they broke into the deserted houses, robbing and wrecking them, decking themselves in ridiculous finery, drinking wildly, until the army became a drunken mob.

But at last the noise of laughter and carouse ceased, and the city sank to rest. The weary soldiers, who for many weeks had slept under the open sky and on the bare ground, slept this night in splendid palaces, on soft couches, and wrapped in silken covers.

But in the middle of the night the cry of fire arose. Soon the city was bright with flames, and morning dawned before they were put out.

But again, when night came, the fire broke out, and not in one place only, but in many. From every quarter, north, south, east, and west, fire burst, until the city was a blazing sea of flame. A strong wind arose, blowing the flames, now here, now there, till palaces and churches, shops and houses, were wrapped in fire, and sank together in piles of charred and blackened ashes.

For two days Napoleon gloomily watched the fearful destruction. Then yielding to the entreaties of his officers, he rode from the burning town, through a whirlwind of flame, a raging hail of sparks, and rolling clouds of smoke.

He took refuge in a palace belonging to the Czar which was beyond the city. But even there the heat of the flames was so great that the stones were hot to touch. Whenever the fire seemed to die down in one place, it kindled again in another. But at last, when four-fifths of the city was a blackened ruin, when there was little left to burn, the flames ceased.

Napoleon then returned and among the ruins he awaited an answer to a letter which he had written to the Czar by the light of the burning city. It was a letter proposing terms of peace. But no answer to it ever came.

Day after day passed. At first there had been food enough for the great army—splendid wines and dainty fare, such as they were little accustomed to, but these soon gave out. Now of bread there was none, and only horseflesh for meat. The Russians had swept the country bare. It was in vain that the French soldiers scoured it in search of food. It was in vain that Napoleon issued proclamations to the peasants, telling them that they would be well paid for anything that they might bring. Their hatred of the French was such that not all the gold in the country could tempt them to Moscow. They would rather have cut off their right hands than have helped Napoleon in the slightest.

The autumn had been unusually warm, the sunny weather had lasted late, but at length it came to an end. A slight snow fell as a warning that the fearful Russian winter was about to begin. It is a winter of keen cold, such as the French had no knowledge of.

They were ill-fed and worse clothed, and in no way fit to endure it.

Again Napoleon wrote to Alexander. Again no answer was returned.

Then, seeing the uselessness and danger of trying to spend the winter in a barren country, hundreds and hundreds of miles from his own kingdom, Napoleon gave the order to march back.

Napoleon had to face defeat. Yet even to himself he would not own it.

"Moscow has been found not to be a good military post," he writes. "It is necessary for the army to breathe in a wider space."

The sick and wounded were left behind, so as not to burden the army. But every soldier was laden with booty. Gold and silver plate, silk and gems were piled in wheelbarrows, beautiful carriages were laden with all kinds of spoil, and a train of Russian prisoners marched bowed beneath heavy loads.

So the march began. But soon the road was strewn with these splendid spoils. Hunger, fearful, gnawing hunger, took hold upon the men. There was nothing to eat but horseflesh. When a horse died, the men fell upon it like hungry wolves, tearing it to pieces. They were ready to kill each other for a few potatoes or a handful of rye. All order and discipline was lost. Many broke from the ranks, and wandering about, seeking vainly for food, perished on the barren steppes.

Harassed by Cossacks, the wretched army still pressed forward. Then came the snow, and with it bitter cold. The snow fell and fell, blotting out the road, blotting out every landmark. Blinded by the whirling flakes, chilled to the bone by cutting winds, the men wandered on, hardly knowing whither. Numbed and frozen, unable to crawl farther, many fell, and the white snow became their winding-sheet. At night perhaps they bivouacked, and in the morning a circle of white mounds alone told where they had lain down to sleep their last sleep.

Pursuing Russians killed those who straggled behind. Often they had no strength to resist. Sometimes even they had no arms, for their muskets would drop from their frozen fingers and be left in the snow.

Yet, through all the misery and cold and famine, a few lived and struggled on. "Smolensk! Smolensk!" they said. That was their goal, the paradise of rest and plenty to which they pressed.

But when Smolensk was at last reached, they found neither rest nor plenty there. The town was as much a ruin as Moscow had been. The stores of food and clothes were exhausted.

After a few days' halt the retreat continued. Near the town of Borisoff the river Beresina had to be crossed by two frail bridges. And here one of the most terrible scenes of the war took place.

While the French crossed they were attacked by the Russians. As men frantic with terror crushed on to the bridges, one of them gave way, and all upon it were thrown into the half-frozen river below. Over the second bridge the French now rushed madly, trampling and killing each other in their haste, shot down in crowds by the Russian bullets. Shrieks of terror and pain filled the air, mingling with the crash and thunder of the Russian guns and the savage cheers of the Russian soldiers. Twelve thousand at least perished at this fearful crossing. The rest continued their march of agony towards Vilna.

RETREAT FROM MOSCOW

Ten days later a miserable, ragged, limping crowd crept into that town. "Remove all strangers from Vilna," Napoleon had written. "The army is not beautiful to look upon just now." But ere the ragged remnant of the once Grand Army had reached Vilna, Napoleon had deserted it. He had heard that there was a rising in Paris. So leaving his soldiers to their misery, wrapped in furs, he hurried as fast as horses could carry him, homeward.

Meanwhile the miserable spectre of an army staggered on, chased by the pitiless Cossacks. At last, in the middle of December, they crossed the Niemen, and found a refuge for a time in and near Königsberg. Of all the magnificent army that had set out to conquer Russia, not twenty thousand famine-stricken men returned.

CHAPTER IX

NAPOLEON
EMPEROR OF ELBA

It should not be forgotten that of all the Grand Army scarcely a sixth were French, and of those the best officers and men returned. So almost at once Napoleon was able to raise a new army. True, most of the new recruits were boys under twenty, but the magic of his name was still so great that they were eager to fight for him. And he had need of all this eagerness, for Prussia, following the example of Spain, and encouraged by the news of Napoleon's awful defeat in Russia, resolved to fight once more for freedom.

Men rich and poor, old and young, flocked to the standard. Ladies brought their jewels, and the Czar of Russia marched to meet his old friend, whom, it is true, he had forsaken, and almost betrayed, at Tilsit. Tears came into the eyes of the old King as he greeted Alexander. "Wipe them," said he; "they are the last tears that Napoleon will ever cause you to shed."

The Prussian leader was Blücher, a rough old man, but brave and loving his country well, and loved by his men, who called him "Marshal Forwards." It was he who, after Jena, held out longest against Napoleon, only surrendering when resistance was useless and hopeless.

The war lasted from April to October. But now Napoleon no longer won victory after victory as he used to do, and at last at the battle of Leipsic he was defeated.

On the 16th of October the battle began. On the 19th Napoleon and his beaten army were streaming across the Elbe, leaving behind them thousands dead, thousands more prisoners, besides hundreds of cannon, stores, and ammunition, and, greatest of all, a mighty empire shattered and crumbling into dust.

Without an army Napoleon could not hold his vast conquests. Without an army he could only be King of the French, and of all his great forces only about forty thousand men hurried towards the borders of France.

All over Europe the nations now began to throw off French yoke. The Dutch and Germans tore the tricolour down, and once more their own standards floated out on the breeze. Everywhere the German fortresses which were held by French soldiers surrendered or were taken.

On the 19th of November Napoleon reached Paris, and here the allies sent to him conditions of peace. Much that he had conquered was to be given back, but not all. The Rhine was still to be the boundary of France. Belgium, Savoy, and Nice also were left to him. But Napoleon did not yet believe in his defeat.

He would not give up any of his conquests. So the allies marched into France, and another war began.

The allies fought, not with France, they said, but with Napoleon. "We thought to find peace before we touched your borders; now we come to find it here."

Many of the people of France had been weary of Napoleon and his wars. But now that the foe had marched into their beloved land, they rose to defend it. Napoleon once more prepared to take the field.

On Sunday, 23rd January, he held a last and splendid reception in the palace of the Tuileries. When the courtiers were gathered, Napoleon walked into the hall with the Empress Marie Louise and his little son, now just three years old. Holding one by either hand, he turned to his court. "Gentlemen," he said, "France is invaded. I go to put myself at the head of the army. I leave to you that which I hold dearest—my wife and son."

Two days later Napoleon said good-bye to Marie Louise. They never saw each other again, for when Napoleon returned to Paris his power was broken, and Marie Louise refused to share the fortunes of a fallen King.

Never perhaps in all his triumphant campaigns had Napoleon shown more his great genius as a soldier than he did now. Nearly always he had fought against armies smaller in numbers or less well drilled than his own. Now he had to fight against far greater numbers, and his soldiers were for the most part young and untrained. Yet still he wrung victories and triumphs from the foe.

But at last, after the war had been flung this way and that, after marches and counter-marches, after taking of towns and burning of villages, until some of the fairest provinces of France had become a desert, the allies began to march on Paris.

Round that fair city, which never since the days of the Maid of Orleans had heard the shouts of a foreign foe, the horrors of war raged. For one long day Prussians filled with bitter hate against their conqueror, half-savage Russians, Austrians, Dutch, people of every country which Napoleon had enslaved, surged in a red circle of fire and death about the city. Then it yielded.

On the 31st of March 1814 the Emperor of Russia and the King of Prussia rode side by side into the city, and passed through the streets filled with people, some sullen and angry, others rejoicing as at a great deliverance, and shouting, "Long live the Emperor Alexander! Long live the King of Prussia!"

Marie Louise had already fled, taking her little son with her. Napoleon, hurrying from the battlefields of Champagne, heard that the fight was over.

"On to Paris!" he cried.

"Sire, it is too late," replied an officer. "Paris has yielded."

Napoleon had been Emperor of half Europe. He had been a king of kings, making and unmaking them at will. In a few years he had built up his mighty empire. In a few months he had lost it bit by bit, until now not even his own capital remained to him. There the allies ruled, and on the 2nd April 1814 the Senate declared that Napoleon had ceased to reign.

But still Napoleon did not believe that all was lost. At Fontainebleau he reviewed his troops. His Old Guard, men who had been with him through every campaign, were still eager to fight for him. "To Paris! to Paris!" they shouted.

But the officers were weary of it all. "We have had enough of war," said one. "Let us not begin a civil war."

So at length, seeing no help for it, Napoleon wrote out and signed his abdication—that is, the paper by which he gave up all claim to the crown of France. "The allied Powers having declared that the Emperor Napoleon is the only cause which prevents peace being brought back to Europe, he, faithful to his oaths, is ready to descend from the throne, to leave France, and even give up his life for the good of his country."

On the 20th of April Napoleon said good-bye to his troops in the courtyard of Fontainebleau. His men loved and admired him still. Tears rolled down their bronzed cheeks, sobs choked them. "I cannot embrace you all," he cried, "but I embrace you in your general." And putting his arms round him, he kissed him. He kissed the standard too, the splendid eagle of France, which had led them so often under burning suns or cloudy skies, through the parching heat of summer or the snows of winter.

Then the fallen Emperor stepped into his carriage and was whirled away southwards. He was an

Emperor still, for the allies allowed him to keep his title. But his empire was only the little island of Elba.

At first, as Napoleon drove through France, the people cheered him on his way. But as he went farther and farther south, where the people had never loved him, and where they now hated him, he was greeted with curses fierce and loud. The peasants cared little for "glory." They only knew that their sons and brothers and fathers had been taken from them, never to return. They knew that the vineyards were unfilled and the fields a barren waste, for the workers lay dead in many a distant land. So they cursed the man whose pride had brought such sorrow and poverty upon them.

At last the anger and hatred of the people grew so great that Napoleon was forced to disguise himself as an Austrian officer to save himself from their fury. And thus he fled southwards until he reached the shore, and there set sail for Elba.

Although the peasants of France had cursed Napoleon as he passed, the people of Elba welcomed him gladly. And here for a little time the great Emperor played at empire.

His empire was not more than ninety square miles in extent. But here Napoleon had his little army of a few hundred men. Here he held court with as great state and ceremony as in the Tuileries, even though his palace was little more than an ordinary country house.

CHAPTER X

NAPOLEON'S LAST BATTLE

Meanwhile the brother of Louis XVI., whom the French had beheaded, was proclaimed King of France. He was not stupid, but he was not clever enough to rule at such a time, when all France, and indeed all Europe, was turned upside down, and full of discontent, every one struggling for something, they hardly knew what.

When the French soldiers, who had been imprisoned in German fortresses, were set free and came back to France, the discontent grew worse. For they, having spent so many years fighting, could not settle down to a life of peace. They longed for their great leader again, and he was soon weary of playing at empire in his little island.

He had been there just eleven months when he made up his mind once more to try his fortune. He escaped from Elba easily enough, and landed near Cannes on March 1st, 1815.

It was near Grenoble that Napoleon met the soldiers sent to stop him. He had with him a little army, for he had brought his soldiers from Elba, though few others had joined. But now he advanced against the enemy alone. "Soldiers," he cried, "if there is one amongst you who desires to kill his Emperor, he can do so. Here I am." And he threw back his coat as if awaiting the blow. But not a weapon was raised. Instead, a shout of "Long live the Emperor!" rang out, and every man marched over to his old leader's side.

At Lyons the Bourbon generals fled, and Napoleon entered the city in triumph. Nay, one of Napoleon's old generals, whom he had called "the bravest of the brave," marched to stop him, vowing to bring his old master back in an iron cage, like a wild beast. But he had not gone far before he too declared for Napoleon, and joined his army.

And so, as on and on Napoleon passed, the little man in the big grey coat, which the soldiers knew and loved, drew them to himself. His army grew larger and larger. Men tore the white cockade of the Bourbons from their hats, and trampled it under foot. Once more the tricolour was everywhere.

In the middle of the night King Louis fled from Paris towards Belgium, and at last, on 19th March, Napoleon once more reached Fontainebleau. The next day he entered Paris.

While the allies were gathered at Vienna, trying to bring order into disordered Europe, they had been suddenly startled by the news that Napoleon had left Elba, and was making his way to Paris. They had not agreed very well, but now this new danger made them forget their quarrels. Quickly they gathered their soldiers, and by June armies were marching against

France from all sides. From Russia, Prussia, Sardinia, Austria, from Holland and Belgium and the German states, and, not least, from Britain, came troops.

But Napoleon did not wait for France to be invaded. He marched northward. He hoped with his usual quick daring to win some splendid battle, and with one stroke shatter the power of the allies, and seat himself again upon the throne of France.

So Napoleon's last campaign was fought in Belgium. The Duke of Wellington commanded a great part of the allied troops which were gathered there, while grim old Blücher led the Prussians. And it was upon the 18th of June, upon the field of Waterloo, that Napoleon made his last stand, fought his last fight—and lost.

The night had been wet and blustry. In the morning rain still fell; the fair fields of Waterloo about the farms of La Haye Sainte and Hougoumont were boggy and sodden, and it was not until nearly twelve o'clock that the battle began. All day long, under a cloudy, stormy sky, it raged. It was a fight of all the nations, and in Wellington's army alone five languages were spoken.

And while at Waterloo the thunder of war roared and crashed, Blücher, with his Prussians, was toiling over rain-soaked roads, his cannon sinking axle-deep in mud, his men splashing and ploughing through deep pools, stumbling wearily onward to join the battle. "We can go no farther," they cried despairingly.

WATERLOO

"We must, my children; I have given my word to Wellington. You would not have me break it," replied Blücher. So they struggled on, but it was late in the afternoon before they reached the battlefield.

The end of the long contest was now near. Napoleon ordered his Old Guard, which he had kept in reserve, to advance. But when he saw them bend and then break and scatter before the British charge, he turned deadly pale. "Why, they are in confusion!" he cried, hardly able to believe it possible. "All is lost. Let us save ourselves."

In utter rout and panic the French fled from the field. The wearied British soldiers left the pursuit to the Prussians. Under the light of the moon and till the dawning of the day the chase went on. For many miles the roads were ghastly, and horrible. Again and again the French tried to take refuge in the villages by the way. Again and again they were driven forth, fleeing before the terrible hurrah of the exultant Prussians, who slaughtered them without mercy.

To France Napoleon fled, tears of anger and despair running down his pale cheeks. On the 10th of June he reached Paris.

There next morning the news that the Emperor had returned alone, and that the great army of France was no more, spread fast.

And now Napoleon learned that, as he was no longer great and successful, the people of Paris did not want him. Of the soldiers who adored him few were left. So once more he abdicated. His second reign, which had lasted only a hundred days, was over.

By his own people Napoleon was ordered to leave Paris—to leave France. But British men-of-war were watching every port, and escape was impossible. So at last he gave himself up to the commander of the *Bellerophon*, and was taken to England. To the Prince Regent he wrote: "I come to seat myself on the hearth of the British people. I put myself under the protection of their laws, which I claim from your Royal Highness as the most powerful, the most constant, and the most generous of my enemies."

Sadly Napoleon watched the shores of France disappear. He never set foot in his adopted land again, never more saw its sunny shores. He was only forty-five, but his life of splendour and excitement was done.

It had been Napoleon's dream to conquer Britain, and add these islands to his empire. Now as a fugitive he was not even allowed to land there. He was kept on the *Bellerophon* until a letter was brought to him which told him that "General Bonaparte" was to be sent to St. Helena, a little island in the South Atlantic.

At Elba, small though his empire was, Napoleon had been still a ruler. There he could still make laws and levy taxes, was still surrounded by an army and a court. At St. Helena he was a prisoner, and a prisoner in a lonely island 2000 leagues from Europe, 900 leagues from the nearest continent.

St. Helena is very small, not more than twenty-one miles all round, and from a distance it looks like a shapeless mass of black rock rising out of the sea. To

Napoleon it seemed a hateful place. And little wonder. After his life of splendour and excitement, it was terrible to be shut away in this lonely island in the middle of the wide ocean. He who had played with kings and kingdoms, making and unmaking them, moving them here and there at will, like chessmen on a board, had now nothing to do. He who had been dreaded by half the world was now of no importance. It mattered not whether he lived or died. So the dreary years dragged on in petty quarrels about petty things, in reading, writing, and chess-playing.

Then after five years the great conqueror lay dying. As he lay, already muttering, and unconscious, a great storm swept the island. It dashed the waves against rocky shore; it bent, broke, and uprooted the willows about his house. But Napoleon lay unheeding it; his wandering mind was dreaming of other days. "France—army—Josephine," he muttered. Then he lay still.

The wind too sank to rest, and when the golden sun of May, shining once more over calm blue waters, slipped beneath the waves, the great restless spirit passed with it.

A few days later, followed reverently by those few of his friends who had clung to him to the last, sharing his lonely exile, he was laid to rest, under the willow trees where he had often sat. British soldiers carried the coffin, upon which was laid the sword and cloak he had worn at Marengo. British soldiers fired a volley and lowered their banners in salute over the grave of their great enemy. And there they left him in a nameless tomb.

Eighteen years later, in the darkness of an October midnight, by the faint light of lanterns, the coffin was once more dug up and carried away to France, with the permission of the British Government.

At the Hôtel des Invalides in Paris it was received by the nobles and the King of France, who, Bourbon though he was, desired to do honour to the great Emperor dead.

"Sire, I present the body of the Emperor Napoleon," said the Prince de Joinville, who, had brought it from St. Helena.

"I receive it in the name of France," replied the King.

So for the last time the greatest soldier the world has ever seen was laid to rest, beside the Seine, among his people, as he himself had wished.

CPSIA information can be obtained
at www.ICGtesting.com
Printed in the USA
LVHW050850021218
598971LV00001B/316/P